FREELAND

FREELAND

poems

LEIGH SUGAR

Alice James Books
NEW GLOUCESTER, MAINE
alicejamesbooks.org

© 2025 by Leigh Sugar
All rights reserved
Printed in the United States

10 9 8 7 6 5 4 3 2 1

Alice James Books are published by Alice James Poetry Cooperative, Inc.

Alice James Books
Auburn Hall
60 Pineland Drive, Suite 206
New Gloucester, ME 04260
www.alicejamesbooks.org

Library of Congress Cataloging-in-Publication Data

Names: Sugar, Leigh, author.
Title: Freeland / Leigh Sugar.
Other titles: Freeland (Compilation)
Description: New Gloucester, Maine : Alice James Books, 2025.
Identifiers: LCCN 2024055252 (print) | LCCN 2024055253 (ebook) | ISBN 9781949944730 (trade paperback) | ISBN 9781949944921 (epub)
Subjects: LCGFT: Poetry.
Classification: LCC PS3619.U3756 F74 2025 (print) | LCC PS3619.U3756 (ebook) | DDC 811/.6--dc23/eng/20241216
LC record available at https://lccn.loc.gov/2024055252
LC ebook record available at https://lccn.loc.gov/2024055253

Alice James Books gratefully acknowledges support from individual donors, private foundations, the National Endowment for the Arts, and the Poetry Foundation (https://www.poetryfoundation.org).

Cover art: "Prison Glass", Scott Gibson, Resin and Mixed Media on Wood, SGibsonArt.com

Ars Poetica   85

III

Revision   89

Notes   93
Acknowledgements   95
Acknowledgements, Too   97

Freeland, Michigan is home to the Saginaw Correctional Facility, a Michigan state prison.

The blank page is not a grid we must adapt to.

It will surely become so, but at what price?

—EDMOND JABÈS
tr. by Rosemarie Waldrop

ARCHITECTURE SCHOOL

I learned to clean the desk before and after laying down the drafting paper to preserve the drafting paper's whiteness. Lead shavings Magic-Erased before they had a chance to mar the blank. The T-square to align the paper to the drafting table and the scale to measure the space between dashed lines. The lines inhaled in the breakroom, steel-ruler scraped and—magic!—erased away. *You don't have to do this*, pressed a classmate I didn't know when I announced my leaving. *Corinthian*, we'd repeat. *Intersecting spaces.* We studied Philip Johnson's Glass House, the perennial favorite. *Seamless integration into the landscape*, we'd praise, then overlay the trace paper to imp our hands to Johnson's Glass. What wonder—to see the thing, and through it.

There is nothing that has nothing to do with this.

—SOLMAZ SHARIF

INHERITANCE

after Natasha Trethewey

In 1920, my grandfather received an American name:
Zucker to *Sugar*, now my own last name.

The Third Reich never tattooed on his forearm
a number. I count myself lucky to have a last name.

Each April, magnolias litter my parents' front yard
before Michigan's spring blizzard exposes its silver face.

My oldest friend's surname is *Blessing*; I know to consider
possible prophecy when giving a name.

At eight, we jarred petals with perfumes and spices
to capture that early spring teasing embrace.

I didn't, back then, know cinnamon from cedar—
those potions turned rancid on shelves, defined *waste*.

These days I scrawl *619754*
on envelopes after a locked-up beloved's last name.

He says, *Leigh, I dream I've forgotten my number
and wake to realize I've forgotten my name.*

AUTOBIOGRAPHY

I wish I was a different story
but I recall that summer, clicking
through late-stage Holocaust photos (bodies
almost unrecognizable as human)
as the most focused, goal-
oriented period of my life: my mother
at the local VA diagnosing post-combat
veterans with early onset dementia
and my father prescribing SSRIs
to affected college students
from his private downtown office suite
while I practiced disappearing
before the start of my junior year.
I'd just passed my driver's test
and spent hours roaming stores
in search of new diet sodas
to trick my body into feeling
full. I didn't succeed,
those months, in becoming
what my family narrowly avoided
in Kraków and Odessa
only decades before, but discovered
in myself the conviction
to pursue any ideal
to its rightful end, a conviction
that, though it would prove nearly fatal
in following years, taught me,
those afternoons hopping
from gas station to supermarket
blasting Gnarles Barkley's "Crazy"
on the red Corolla's radio,
I could conjure a world
and, of my own volition,
make it true.

ECLIPSE BEFORE SEEING YOU IN PRISON

Echoing light
is a punctum for meditation.

What irreverent law,
the cosmos: birds circle aimlessly
in false dusk.

To rest in a chosen home
is the assumption of freedom.

With wrap-around, blackout goggles
and pin-holed, cardboard boxes

even a solar eclipse is bound.

SECURITY

OPEN GATE ONE step in

put your keys and your ID on the table walk through
      the machine whoops

           take your belt off try again

      it smells in there by the way OK GATE TWO

                                  grab your things

come in I even set up fans and everything but man it's awful like
      a bunch of 'em forgot to shower

                set your things down on the counter sit down

         take off your shoes
              and socks show me your feet

      turn your shoes upside down and knock 'em together

              you staying with family
              or somethin'? stand up lift your tongue say *ahhhh*

                      turn around lift
              your hair you come a long way

      pull out your pockets

inmates
       they get three meals
              and a roof and a bed

          me I get paid I been here twenty-one years

                           I get seniority
         on holidays this year I got Christmas
                    and Thanksgiving

I hope I get out on time today ready
                  grab your ID
                      and locker key I ain't kiddin'
    it's awful in there OPEN GATE TWO

I been holdin' my breath all day step out

                 arms out like a airplane

       spread your legs

                what I don't get is why
                      you choose to come here

I pretend I am an anthropologist when I lift my hair and tongue to show I hide no drugs or weapons behind my ears or in my mouth.

VISITING STANDARDS

Four states have conjugal visits
Michigan is not one of them

In fantasies about your first night home
We imagine ourselves on a wood floor

Your body unfit for a mattress
My body accustomed to coming up against a hard edge

Give me a thick reason to curse away
Your clothes, you wrote in a letter

Crayon drawing rejected
For UNIDENTIFIABLE MATERIAL RESIDUE

An officer searches photos
For nipples or genitals

An officer searches your body like an envelope
Before we meet again in the room of infinite goodbyes

We pour food from the vending machine
Onto paper plates

It is easier to spot contraband
Displayed against a white background

[A NUMBER IS JUST A NAME.]

A name is just a room you can't get out of.

        It matters who mans the camera
        whether you can touch my thigh or run your fingers through my hair
        or if I can lay my head on your shoulder.

Before you I thought the body a prison

                and the mind, Foucault's panopticon.

        Now I know you might wait two hours to pee
        if you sign up to use the bathroom during count time
        when officers cannot supervise you
        because they are too busy counting other bodies.

(Note accompanying a white V-neck T-shirt—*619754*
printed along its body-side bottom hem—
wrapped in a clear plastic garbage bag
an officer hands me to put in the coin-operated locker
before moving through security to see you:

> *I wore this sweaty and aching*
> *after lifting weights)*

[I ONLY EVER SEE HIM IN A JUMPSUIT]

and I tell him I wish he could see me
in the dress I'll wear to my cousin's wedding,
layered gauze, loose, dusty blue, ruffled mid-
thigh hem, braided straps rising to a halter,
flowers appliqued on the chest—

I wish you could see me, too, he says.
You should've seen me at my appeal,
I wore a tan suit, white, oxford shirt, sky-
blue tie, brown, round-toed derby shoes.
I look good in suits, he says.
I looked good.

[THE PRISON PHOTOGRAPHER MAKES HIS ROUNDS,]

walking from tiny table to tiny table, asking who wants a Polaroid to commemorate the visit. I buy a photo ticket in the waiting room vending machine to get a picture by this bunkie or friend. We keep fucking it up —a blink at the flash; a strand of hair in the mouth; a last-minute glance away from the insta-camera's snap and its uneditable proof of err. How to cheat; to stretch a ticket into time. Time into time. How to spend more time holding each other and posing. Posing, holding.

FANTASY

Do I stay in the car or do I wait for you in the waiting room where I've been returning all these years to visit   Do I call ahead or do I trust that everything's proceeded smoothly   Do I bring a change of clothes for you   What color T-shirt do you want   V-neck or crewneck   What size jeans   What fit   What fit will be in style in ten years   What brand of underwear   Do you still like black boxer-briefs   Sneakers or boots   High or low-cut socks   Should I bring a snack   Is a bagel with cream cheese OK   How about fruit salad   How long since you've eaten a strawberry   I'll bring some with pineapple and melon   Where will you emerge from   What door   What will you be wearing when I first see you   What do they do with your jumpsuits   How quickly do they land in someone else's locker   Are you restricted in how many bags you carry out   What will you do with all your books   Will you give away your shoes and gym shorts   Will you have had time to shower   Will anyone help you carry your things   Can I stand to greet you   Do I sign anything   Can we kiss   What does the officer say to you   Does the officer wish you luck   How tight is my stomach   How steady are your hands   Are you nervous to ride in a car   Are you nervous to be alone with me   Do you want to buy something   Do you want to hold money   Do you want to turn on the radio   Can we stay in the parking lot while we decide what to listen to   Can we kiss in the parking lot   Will we want to   Will we be able to stop   Will we call your family   Will we have plans for the day   What is the weather   Will you roll down your window as we drive out through the gate   Will you look ahead   Will you turn your neck to see the prison shrink behind you   Do you want to stop for coffee   Do you want to choose your order or should I   How does it feel   What do we say   Where do we go

ode to phone sex

after Ocean Vuong

because no one told us
we could pour
this decade-long night
into our stranded bodies
and call it
home

        go ahead—call
        an ache
        into a name

    answer absent
    a body
    to hold

            take time
            between two fingers

this now will live
until someone destroys
the evidence

        now

come
forge a world
that can never hold us
together

       the voice hums
       a wave warm
       and blood-close

a moment folds
under fences
crowded
with loneliness

    listen: miles
    are just blankets
    for wet skin

*Square room with child-sized tables.
Armless plastic chairs. Windows facing
a barbed-wired, fenced-in courtyard.
Vending machines. Cellophane-
wrapped hamburgers. Plastic spoons.
Paper napkins.*

REPRESSION

A smile, when the officer commands I stop

touching you. The space between shame

and pleasure shorter than the scythe-

shaped stretch of shoulder

revealed when my shirtsleeve slips off

the me whose swift hands leave your neck to right the slip

then return to my own lap. I sag,

guilty, still, still under the camera.

We resolve to resist resistance:

you are you and you are in here

and in here we take what we can get—

some touch is better than no touch.

Next time I will wear a shirt that stays

in its place.

BONE TUMOR (flashback)

I knew it was something bodies could do, disobey—
a girl a grade above had died that fall
of the cancer I was being tested for in winter,
and one the grade below lay in the hospital with leukemia;
she'd been showing up to ballet with bruises
up and down her legs for months before the diagnosis—
but didn't know *my* body could, or that it would,
however benignly. The numbers said it was inevitable:
one in a thousand worked out to one per grade
in that overfilled high school where thrumming masses
bottlenecked hallways passing from Spanish
to biology to gym. I couldn't know, then,
the case from my class would come the following year,
also in the bone but spreading, hers, to other places.
The X-ray showed my bone looked moth-eaten
where my marrow should have been. The doctor said
I couldn't dance, or run, or lift a ceramic mug
for fear the bone might break, the break might spread
malignancy if any malignancy existed; they couldn't know
until they saw it, not even after biopsy, that big cylinder
chamber above the long syringe going in and in.
Instead of ballet class, I'd sit for hours every day
practicing piano—scales and etudes
were things I could get fluent in. Improve.
The surgery was quick. I was benign, or, at least, my bone
was. They filled it with synthetic stuff and closed me up.
I stayed in the hospital until the drainage bag
stopped draining, a plastic straw connecting from within
my arm to a little plastic pouch collecting blood
and whatever yellow-y liquid was also coming out.
The only time I cried was when they pulled it out—
I've never felt anything stranger
than the extraction of a foreign object from deep inside
my bone—that inhalation, the empty-leaving
sucking tunnel where part of me had been before.

ONTOLOGY OF MY ASSUMED IMMUNITY

after Nicole Sealey

White my first blankets in infancy; white the keys
of my first piano scales; white the lilies after which
a childhood friend is named, whose petals

her seamstress mother embroidered with white thread
on white wedding dresses for brides who'd later bring them
to cleaners to be restored to their white glory. White my teeth

and white the car I drive to arrive here. Here,
administration is concerned about white powder
substitutes slipping in via gummed, manila seals.

New policy mandates white-enveloped white-paper
letters, forgets white deviance, too, cloaks in white.
In school when I misspelled a word or held my pen

too long on paper, I corrected with white-out. Now
in letters to him I'll strike through or scribble out
the mistake, lament the errant marks on the once white

page. No white-coated doctors, no bone-white pills,
no white picket fences, no fresh-pulled milk, no fresh-
laid quilt of snow can treat the warping blue

of time-bloated days. On visits he white-knuckles
the back of my chair, my hand. I tell him to squeeze
until our blood bottlenecks, stalls. Our hands blanch white.

Individual mustard packets. Four Bibles and three children's Bibles. Pencil sketch of Dora the Explorer. Pencil sketch of Jesus on the cross.

BUYING A VENDING CARD BEFORE THE VISIT

: Can I help you with that?

: OK, first use your dollar—

: Yeah, just a one-dollar bill—

: You put it in the machine and press that button—

: OK, now you have your card—

                                                                : Yeah—

: Take that card—

: See the top—

: Yeah, so, you put it back in the machine—

                                                                : Yep—

: With the gold side up—

                                                                : Yeah—

: And then put your money in—

                                                                : Yep—

: When you're done—

: Are you done—

                                                                : Yep—

: Push that button again—

                                                                                 : Yeah—

: Somebody helped me my first time, so, I figure—

: You can't use it at any other facilities—

: Nope, if you have money left on it and they move—

                                     : That's how they get us, you know—

: It has a number on it you can write in—

: To the company to request the money back—

: I got some money back, but it took a while—

: At the other place the money expires—

                           : I visited two guys, but too long passed, so I had to reactivate—

                    : They let me reactivate, but you have to write them—

                  : Otherwise that's how they get your money—

                              : That's how they get us—

                         : That's how they get our money—

: Well, somebody helped me my first time, so, I figured—

CORRECTIONS

I have wanted to leave you there
and never return. Never answer another OFFENDER
CALL, never again disconnect at the 15-minute limit
that leaves me alone and flush from your imagined
presence after phone sex, never again take mouthwash
at the stop sign, dab oil on my wrists and neck
before the gate in preparation for our sanctioned hello
kiss. Never again ask to use the bathroom and, upon standing,
be told to leave because the wet spot on my pants,
because your fingers, for hours, playing in the soft place
between my palm and thumb left me
pink and dripping, unfilled. That is, if my body
can't be our body unsurveilled,
I want my body to be only my body again.

//

I want your body to be only my body
and not state property to be held and taxed.
To help, you drew a shirtless portrait
of yourself for me and called it prayer.
Where does one display a verse like that?
The body is the prison of the mind
and the mind of the soul, etc. The page
inerts the body—stasis foisted upon stasis.
I only ever want to move, afraid of fester,
of staying, of being made to stay. You say
you keep my photos in a folder; mine of us
remind me of... I don't want them displayed
on my walls at home. If I can't see you
my mind can't replace your face with a cage.

//

So I don't confuse your face with a cage
I wield my mind as a scythe to cut the years
as if the years revolve around my desire,
an impossible thread from me to you pulled taut
across the country. When I watch a couple
holding hands while walking home at night,
I wrestle my memory to create a memory
of walking home with you. When I pretend
I can walk away whenever I want,
I know I'm claiming false power to soften
the wanting what I cannot have—your hand,
a home, some place to walk together.
When I feel stuck, I imagine you moving in circles.
Then I walk five miles in straight lines.

//

I walk miles travelling in straight lines
to remind myself I'm allowed to move
from here to there no matter where
there or *here* may be. I've crossed the country
a dozen times in the time you've been away.
In the time you have left, one could start
and finish a law degree *and* a PhD
and still have months to spare.
Why marry myself to my imagination
of a future you and me? No one asked me
to put myself inside a box, least of all, you.
Is cruelty the box, or is the box the shape
we need to have before we draw, then build,
then walk right through an open door?

//

Then walk right through an open door,
I dare myself when I get scared
to stay. I've seen how staying people sink
into the floor, the locked windows,
displaced inside an endless placement.
How to build a life in places built
to arrest life? A small child slams
against a sliding glass security door
upon seeing his father step inside.
Why are there no blooming fields or skies
inside these poems? You sent me roses
once, or rather, your mom did. They lived
until they didn't. The flowers turned to
rotting stems inside a grime-streaked vase.

//

Rotting stems outside my grime-streaked window
signal another winter has come, is going,
despite not asking for permission. As time passes
we approach your out-date but we lose
the months to age. I count my grays each week
and pray to find a god to pray to. On visits
we see couples joining hands and bowing heads
with Bibles spread across their laps. *The Ministry
Fund on S&P is up today,* we laugh, and prop a Bible
up across our laps to block the cameras
from our grasping hands. *Perhaps I should be grateful
just to have a love at all,* I appeal, in case a god
requires such a statement to configure.
I'm bored of waiting, I'll say if one appears.

//

I'm tired of waiting, I say to no one.
He says he still remembers what it's like
to drive, to swim, to run without a shirt,
to shirtless lay outside and look up at the stars.
I describe to him the fruit I eat for breakfast
and the strangers I nod to on the sidewalk
so he can know my days and fill the space
between where I live and where he sleeps.
I'm sorry for all the poems I have not written.
Silence is no way to elegize absence,
no way to keep an absence alive.
He says he wakes up hard from dreaming
our togetherness. I smile and don't tell him
I don't dream about him anymore.

//

I don't dream about him anymore,
don't picture that he warms the bed for me
at night before I slip inside, don't feel
his thick arm wrap around to steady me
on dark tracks passing underground. No, I don't
pull out two mugs for tea then put one back,
I don't imagine calling him to ask
which he thinks a better word for patience:
fossilize or *cocoon*. I don't see collared
shirts in stores and wonder how he'd look in them:
blue or green, or black, crisp-creased slacks,
a narrow tie striped white and gray, a leather belt.
I trained myself to not imagine him at all, not
write ourselves into a life that doesn't yet exist.

//

Through letters, we wrote ourselves into existence.
Forged a shared history amidst the void.
Became—ourselves, each other—characters
for the other's story. *It's too much pressure
to be your symbol of freedom*, I said, and knew
I was projecting. I don't know how to love you
other than to tell you of my days, my meals,
everything you cannot see. What if it's not enough?
What if writing you my life is a distraction
from some other writing I should, could,
would be writing? I'm afraid to be a woman
waiting. I've always lived with hunger.
I'm more afraid of your presence. Afraid
of what will happen when the lack is gone.

//

The lack happens at family dinners,
in the car driving to and from anywhere,
in the shower, the body and its bony cage
of law. I used to think my life was a performance
and the audience appeared according to my will
whenever I did something beautiful—
my hair perfectly curling while making the bed;
my flirting smile at the newly walking baby
on the street. Now, I know you can't see me
when I'm not beside you in the place I hate.
I really hate it, going there. Freeland.
Where people fish off the highway overpass.
It's not the strip search but its everydayness.
When you leave, what will you bring home?

       //

When we leave for the first time
I'll have to drive, but maybe we will stop
for gas and you can hold the card and pay.
I don't mean to patronize, just—how long
has it been? You behind the wheel
on the highway driving home? Notice
the gas gauge creep toward a quarter tank?
Pull into a station? Pull your wallet
from your pocket? Swipe your card, enter
your zip code? Choose a gas grade,
fill your own car with your own money?
This is what I think to call freedom: you
paying for our gas, me in the passenger seat
waiting, waiting for you to return.

//

Waiting for him to return, I search for pleasure
in other bodies. We agree this is only reasonable.
One body was so attractive my teeth hurt.
The man looked like Brad Pitt, who I'd never liked
before. This is what I told him later: we walked
to my place down the middle of the empty midnight
street holding hands. I also told him about the sex
but it was the street, its emptiness, the midnight
walking, that haunted him most. I don't feel
guilty. I want to forget his reality,
the one where he carries his own toilet paper
to the bathroom. I don't understand most of what
goes on there, where he is, and why. Sometimes
I need to not understand in a way that makes sense.

//

I need to know:
What is the worst thing you've ever done?
I can pull him up on the state's database
anytime and read about his case.
What can he ever know about me?
Not that I forget to remove my keys
from the lock outside my door; not that I sneeze
when I look directly at the sun; not
that I used to steal candy from the bulk bins
at the organic co-op, stashing handfuls
of malt balls and chocolate-covered cherries
in my pockets. I didn't want to pay,
to legalize my craving. If no one ever saw,
I thought it didn't count. I was never caught.

//

If you were never caught is not a game
we play. We play card games from the stash
in the visiting room and marvel at our chance
meeting. We wouldn't have loved if not in here.
If I wasn't caught when I was caught,
I'd still have gotten caught, he means. *I'd do it*
all again for you, he says. I used to catch
fireflies in jars to keep beside my bed.
I wanted to see wings, but in the morning
they were always dry and coiled. I like
the keeping part. The part of me that feeds
on order is relieved to always know where he is.
In five years, he will still be here.
In five years, we have never been alone together.

//

Because we cannot be alone together,
I learn to be together with myself
alone. I hold myself to fall asleep
and know it's not him holding me.
The world out here extends beyond my mind
extending itself to him. I know I am not guilty
for enjoying the sky, the stars, the moon's light
and not thinking of his view—obstructed
by floodlights. I walk, I dance, I run, I learn
how the language I was born into can't
disappear a law already enacted, not even
when uttered with love, and I am OK.
Words only sometimes feel imprisoning.
The sun rises and I only sometimes think of him.

//

Sun unlocks day and I picture you,
awake in your cell with your bunkie, planning
your next workout, how many hundreds of pounds
you will lift or resist against; you, lunching
at chow hall, piles of conglomerated meat
baked into slices; you, studying your case
at the law library; you, writing me by hand
a hundred letters; you, locked in your cell
for count time three times every day.
Alone, we silent ask if love is leaving a part
of oneself with your love whenever you're apart.
In the visiting room I try to reconcile the you
I love with the jumpsuited you beside me.
I confess I want to leave and leave you there.

INHERITANCE TOO

[photo 1]:

    my maternal grandmother in Detroit, 1940, baking cake sweetened with bananas to welcome home

[photo 2]:

    the man who would become my grandfather, stationed in London as a pharmacist, comfortable and safe and smuggling steaks for friends, hiding bottles of vodka in his medicine case to share with comrades (he looks barely twelve, smiling

                  under his garrison cap).

[(WHAT WERE YOU THINKING]

when you held it, cool weight heavy in your sixteen-year-old grip, muzzle gaping like a hooked fish inches from the checkout girl's marble eyes, the shouts, your relief at her compliance, the open cash drawer, the open car door, its open sunroof, and then the years and years and years and years rolled out before you then stacked up, one on top of the other, like the cash you'd stash after a deal, like a deck of cards in the visiting room game basket, like the jeans in the closet of your childhood bedroom your mother still keeps pristine—)

The word is a wall outside of which no body can stand

GRAND UNIFIED THEORY OF MASS INCARCERATION, OR, HOW TO LEAVE

It's something to turn away from—
a cabinet filing lives to review
or retrieve at your convenience.

Learn the game: blink to erase
a body into oath into shadow into stone
into shackle into chattel into cage.

You can be paid to shape a nameless mass.
In the image of a nation's myth
a system creates a body to abandon.
In the image of a nation's myth
you can be paid to shape a nameless mass

into shackle into chattel into cage.
A body into oath. Into shadow. Into stone.
Learn the game. Blink to erase—

or retrieve, at your convenience—
a file cabinet holding lives to review.
It's something to turn away from.

A child runs into the glass door behind which their father sits. Synthetic Christmas tree. Polaroid camera. Cheeto-dust-coated fingertips. Three red LEGOs in a yellow bin.

FREELAND: AN ERASURE

The world is the world.
—Srikanth Reddy

Day forms night over again in fine glass sheets of blue.

The unit is.

See my body, a shifting silver ministry.

Hell kicked over two days ago; ground officers shaped time into this shape.

Our country's a scene in a movie.

A banger, a MasterLock, an extension cord, respectively.

Sit inside your anything beautiful, your anything song.

It's not so bad.

//

Natural life swings wide, turns physical.

Like a good family, we fetch water, mind honor, write letters.

Dream the loose blue tank top, the ceaseless white.

The mirror rejects your reflection, citing *inappropriate content*.

Dayroom immigrants melt into threads of crucial affiliations.

My father's contaminating line shares a bottle with me.

A grin strains, readjusts, speaks an earthy state.

Cleaned up, you can culture a facility refund.

　　　//

The U.S. approached with coffee and a bed.

Tired, I read, ate.

Tomorrow the cages will wait for their respective dogs.

A hot bus glows with peppers, tomatoes, carrots—a premeditated drive-through art.

The origami engineering is a dream.

Hanging from stardust, the installed concertina almost winking.

My window opens to a very small wire.

Beyond the glowing retrospect, a region shines.

//

As a boy, I could hop a chain-link fence.

I breathed snow.

I convinced the kids from school the sky was my mother.

Here, men play heroes to crickets in the yard.

I used to run mountains, but I've never been on a train.

I've gotten used to the warehouse.

The world waterfalls to a future beyond this grass and dirt.

I've learned a person can still grow in a pool of gray.

      //

Possible futures pour like loud blues from too-small headphones.

I know mine is not murdered.

Let me say it again: I know my future is not murdered.

A wrench heavies through, tumors hours into years.

Divorced from peers, entire legs become teeth, then clamshells, then solid crystal.

I see people freeze, then melt, then freeze.

I would like to ask for home's number, take her to dinner sometime.

Sixty each: pullups, chin-ups, and pushups—premeditate a glistening *out there*.

//

Not even Eliot or Pound approach the melancholy weapon of the punitive farm.

In profile, I separate from this justice.

Tattoo economy pens my skin into a letter.

Dear anyone.

Distorted paintings brush against the sentence.

Any box will logic a soul into a numbered life.

I don't know what I look like.

I picture my sister running and playing games when my mind is being searched.

//

Even inside this U-shaped slab, I don't worry about my safety.

I lock my life to a flower pressed between books.

My mom and dad and brother and sister and grandparents and friends all have names.

Bodies and names as infinite as fields of corn.

So do I.

I tell them to sit in the grass and look up at storms and melting lights.

Look and look because they can.

I know one day I will be held again.

      //

Some days I walk and talk with other men.

Some days we sprint and lift ourselves until we flower into muscle.

We package our adult selves into small metal walls.

We don't say we feel like paper in a fountain.

Instead, *Dear fish*, we write.

Dear kids and bare skin and crickets outside the fence.

Dear Cheerios, dear cherries, and pretzels, and chocolate chips, and chocolate bars with orange in them. Dear iced tea and making out. Dear school. Dear New Hampshire and California and New York and Detroit. Dear barbershops and the shape of clothes not blue:

I remember you.

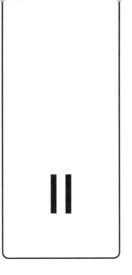

What is lost?

—REGINALD DWAYNE BETTS

SELF ON PSYCH HOLD IMAGINES FUTURE SELF AFTER PSYCH HOLD

I will stop doing everything I don't want to do
like sleeping in past eight or getting bored
in the drugstore self-checkout line.
Ants curling in synchronized task
don't impress me anymore.
The full moon looks like a raspberry,
a five-year-old declares, and this is my magic.
Nothing is not in conversation
with everything. Beneath the clouds
a mountain lion traces a body into a mind
afraid of dying. The pause between inhale
and exhale disintegrates in space, reassembles
as another gray hair. Get all the air out
to sing a little longer. An unwritten letter
teases an ache from the ether. The unopened
prison letter teases out letters for this poem.
Let me hold off transcendence
for another tomorrow. I don't not want to die,
just not yet.

PHENOMENOLOGY

If you cover one eye

      you can fit a whole person

           in the space

   between

         your thumb

  and

pointer finger.

PHONE CALL WITH THE NOW FORMER BELOVED, NOVEMBER 2016

: I'm reading a Martha Nussbaum essay right now called "Love and the Individual." I'm halfway through, but I think you'd like it. She talks a lot about Greek philosophy. She like, writes about it, and she's talking about this woman who wrote a story about a woman who had an experience with love, trying to figure it out. I'm pretty sure she's all three women. But she makes a point of saying, *I found an essay on the floor of an office I just rented, and I don't know who wrote it,* but it has the same title as the one I was going to write... It's comparison and contrast between different views of love... One is like, *Everything is general, and every loving person is an extension of a universal value, so it's all replaceable.* And another says, *It's entirely personal, and virtues of another person are built upon a history.*

: Did you ever get the book I sent you?

: No, there was no mail on Election Day or yesterday, Veterans Day.

: What's the climate there?

: Pretty cold, I woke up and it's frosty—

: I don't mean... I mean the attitude, the feeling.

: Oh! Everything's—you mean—? There's a lot of talk, I guess, myself, I'm past the initial shock. Everybody was talking about it for a while and then it was like, whatever. One joke that keeps coming up is that everybody keeps telling my bunkie, *You're going back to Mexico!*

: No, what I was saying though is like, 'cuz there's been sort of like a, um, a split between people who are like, *If you supported [   ] then don't talk to me, I don't want to interact with you*, versus like, *Well, the reason this happened is because we're not talking to each other*, and ... I don't know, I mean, there's some pretty, I think that like, the news outlets that you are seeing, or you have access to right now, like, I think, I'm probably seeing different, or more, like on-the-ground stuff, and one thing is like what this government can actually do, and the other is like, a certain type of [   ] supporter is now emboldened to think a certain kind of language is acceptable, so I have connections, friends on social media, people talking about very—incidents that have happened to them in the past three days that are directly the result of... like, people thinking it's OK to follow an East-Asian-presenting girl on the street saying, *Do you speak English? Do you speak English? Go back to your country*. I mean, these are people I know, these are people I went to high school with, so, it's kind of, yeah. Like—

: I think there's going to be some government, emotional fallout from this, I mean, it'll be interesting. I mean, in terms of practicality, I think the only thing moving forward is... OK, so if people in general really need to be able to decide for themselves, to say, we need to find our own way to make things happen. [pause] You OK?

[[You have [pause] sixty seconds remaining.]]

: Call me back.

[[Hello, this is a prepaid debit call from [pause] ____ [pause] a prisoner at the Michigan Department of Corrections Saginaw facility. If you feel you are being victimized or extorted by this prisoner, please contact GTL Customer service at ____. To accept this call, press 0.]]

[[button sound]]

[[This call is from a corrections facility and is subject to monitoring and recording. Thank you for using GTL.]]

: OK, so I probably sense a certain feeling of responsibility that you don't feel because your outlets are very limited, in terms of what you could do in this situation, I mean, I don't want to make assumptions, but I mean, you couldn't even vote, so when I hear you talk about it, nothing you're saying is incorrect, but it's not the tone of how I'm thinking, because for me, it's not like, "people need to do x," it's like, what do I need to do?

: What are you doing today?

: I don't know, schoolwork.

: How's that going?

: I mean, it's hard to focus, but I think it's gonna be fine, but, uh, what was I gonna say, oh, uh, I was walking yesterday... I wrote it in part of my essay, so I was walking out of class, and there was a big rally coming through, and I was crossing Sixth Ave., which is a really big street, and I was crossing and I had a walk signal and I was looking in the direction of where the rally was going, and a biker ran into me, like, a biker hit me—

: Are you OK?!

: Yeah, I'm fine, I mean, it coulda been really bad actually! And he didn't... I mean, he didn't hit the middle of me, he like hit, I don't even know how it happened... it was either right in front of me or beside me... brushed my side... but it wasn't like, I felt the wind in my hair, he like, ran into me, and it was like, really bizarre, and he just kept going, and then he looked back, and yelled, *Sorry!* And then *I* said, *Sorry!*

: I do the same thing, I mean, my bunkie will run into me and then I'll say—

: No, but he ran into me on a bike! In the middle of a street!

: You wrote about it in your paper?

: Yeah, kind of, it just seemed like another thing to throw into the mix of the week.

: Are you getting a cold?

: No. Are you?

: Yeah.

[[car horns]]

: Do I sound like I am?

: A bit.

: Maybe you were projecting.

 Clarify who is who among your friends, *I used to ask, again and again.* I can't keep the faces and names straight. We all dress the same, *he always forgave.*

[AT THE GROUP HOME WHERE I WORK]

a woman gives a writing workshop.
She tells the children she had been abused,
too, and then we all write poems.

One girl says she does not write, but thinks
life is a kite, and when the string is cut,
by someone or something, that is death.

Transcribing, I ask, *What happens*
if it gets caught in a tree?
Then*, she says, you get to walk a tightrope*
to the moon.

FANTASY

Parents live with their children unless their children aren't safe with them in which case children live with the adults most perfectly equipped to manage and love each child uniquely. Water is clean and everywhere. Public schools are fully resourced and meet the learning and social needs of every student regardless of where they come from and what they look like. Everyone who wants to goes to college and everyone knows the most important people are the trash collectors and janitors and mail deliverers so no one thinks that people who go to college are more valuable than people who don't. People addicted to alcohol or opioids or meth or scripts or gambling or porn or food or hunger find healthy alternative behaviors so ful-filling there's no need to ever return. Food is free and homes are free and clothes are free and no one takes more than they'll use and everyone uses an amount that satisfies them but doesn't in-fringe upon others' needs. Diseases have cures and doctors to cure them, and there is no hierarchy of who gets what care when. People only die when they've lived long enough to give love and receive love and learn as much as they're capable of, and then when it happens it is without pain or cost. Everyone plays card games and kickball and catches fireflies (and lets them go). Cells are only what keep bodies and plants alive. Officers are well-being officers, and officers of health and the environment and bees and drinking water, and they are not officers. Solitary confinement is when you choose to enter a room filled with sunlight. No one puts you there but you. No one keeps you there. No limits to what you can make with your hands. No doubt that your story is important.

[MY FRIEND WILL IS TRYING TO GET BETTER AT WRITING.]

He says Pound said you should
be able to describe a tree
so that a person could use the description as a map
and identify, in a grove amongst other trees,
the exact one described.

He also says it seems important
that a writer be able to describe the sky, and asks
if I can describe the sky.

How to look and know
you can never ever
see the whole.

THE COMMUNE IN SANTA CRUZ
for Vishwa Nath and Sudhir Dass

A community elder takes to me, requests a dining room lunch date. *My life is a bag of marbles*, he admits. *Pretty, and ultimately insignificant.* Tells me he wrote poems until his guru told him poetry would not bring him enlightenment. In his twenties, he tripped on mushrooms in the Pacific Coastal Ranges. *Walking back to the car*, he says, *the mountain said to me: All worlds are words I have heard before.*

DEFINE FANTASY

(planting tomatoes / voting / riding a bike)

A dream of the future—

(lips to your neck just inside / the door still / open
my thighs / open around your knee / bent toward the wall
behind / me your hands pressed against / the wall chest
to chest / to thigh / tongue / inside
arching / a moan from / somewhere / is a bed / we don't make it
to / the couch / the floor / me on top is how / I pin you
down / your hands above your head / craning
to see / me / unbutton / yours / already open /
my legs / struggle / sigh / around
you /
your hips)

What future—

(my hair is still brown /
I am still fertile)

The one we might live as our own.

(why would my fantasy include arguing /
about whose turn it is / to change /
the empty / toilet paper roll?)

TO BE

If *the girl is sick* / Spanish knows / it is not forever: / la chica *está* inferma / not / *es* inferma.

We have a word / to say / the door [   ] open.

The gate [   ] locked. / The camera [   ] watching. / You [   ] wearing a jumpsuit. / We [   ] not allowed to touch. / The room [   ] too full. / The fence [   ] all around us.

The sky [   ] sea-glass blue. / The cream [   ] sweet. / The tide [   ] high. / The flower [   ] in bloom.

(Found scribbled on a Post-it while cleaning
out the car:

Correction = *rote core erect tore tone torn
ion con   tine cite
rector toon   corn coo
necrotic   nice tire
trio note   not tin
net rice   cero
crone coin   rein ire
ice cot rite iron err rot*)

IN WHICH THE PRISONER PAINTS HIMSELF AS REMBRANDT
after Rainer Maria Rilke

The artist in the painting has no hair
and wears a t-shirt and baggy slacks—
perhaps the untucked jumpsuit
of the artist rendering the artist.

The Rembrandt portrait on the wall is black
and white, as is the painting of the artist
painting Rembrandt, the conceiving artist perhaps
without access to color. Who is painting
who, and what?

If the artist paints, without color,
an artist painting on a blank wall
in implied full spectrum, does he not
have color with which to paint, and a blank
wall on which to paint it?

Thin brushes, fat brushes, half-
used paint tubes strewn across the wood floor,
tackle box open and filled
with more paints and brushes, and a side table
with a lamp and boots and a can
or candle, it is hard to tell—

cloaked in robes, Rembrandt's perfectly
shaded head, hair emerging
from a skull wrap, a seeing eye
and one still coming alive
under the artist's hand.

The artist is balanced on one foot, sinking
into the couch cushions, the other knee
propping a paint pallet between couch

and wall... does he not now,
with canvas on which to paint a wall,
and an imagined artist with color and tools
and solitude and space, possess color, tools,
solitude, space?

The artist reaches
towards the final quadrant of the portrait's face—

RECURRING DREAM

I sit down to write a love poem and end up writing a letter to my daughter,
the daughter I don't yet have:

Dear Daughter,

*There is a prison in Louisiana called Angola.
Angola, after the country the slaves who were brought to Louisiana to pick cotton
came from. At Angola Prison, there are chain gangs, and a rodeo, too!*

Love,

Your mom

And then I teach her to count.

IN THE WAITING ROOM (flashback)
after Elizabeth Bishop

The day after Thanksgiving,
November 28th, 2014, I went to Jackson, Michigan.
There are three prisons there,
and I arrived at the right one at the right time, 9:42 am,
to get a good spot in the visitors' line.
There were already people outside
the main entrance. A corrections officer
poked his head out the door, told us, *Come back
at 9:45*, so we hugged the exterior walls
and became invisible.
Three minutes later he was ready.
We went inside.
I wrote my name on a list
and before the officer took my ID
and searched my body, I waited
in the waiting room.
In the waiting room there were no women
with awful, hanging breasts
or even *National Geographic* images of them
but there was a tickertape newsfeed
on the flat-screen TV
mounted above the lockers visitors use
because we can't bring anything inside.
The man on the screen warned me to watch
for a missing girl with blonde hair;
she's seven, maybe twelve.
There were lots of other people in the waiting room:
there were grown-up people and babies
(they had normal heads)
and in-between people too.
Some of them watched the man
on TV and some of them sat
in the blue plastic bucket seats bolted

to the ground and some of them stood
at the lockers fumbling with coins and keys
to lock late-fall-Michigan belongings inside—
parkas and wallets, knitted hats and mittens.
I heard, *Where's daddy?*
A girl pressed her face to the double-plated glass
separating our waiting room from the security room
(there's another room after that,
and then another where the prisoners wait).
She had two dark curly pigtails and a white party dress
with big blue flowers on it—hydrangeas, maybe?
(She'd dressed up for the occasion.)

I heard my dad yell,
BE *CAREFUL*! and suddenly we were all
everyone in the waiting room
(even the officer and the man on TV)
we were all on our dad's laps licking ice cream.
And the ones without dads were on their dad's laps licking ice cream
we were on the beach pulling kites
in the park playing tag
on the floor climbing bellies (mountains);
they're reading us books,
the dads, there's a sea of them, of books,
a sea of books, and a sea of dads.

The picture on the screen was one of us
(or it could be)
it was certainly not a *them.*
He wore a Tigers baseball cap,
his eyes far from his nose,
his ears peeked out from under his hat,
he was not smiling,
and, instead of his shirt, we saw text
line the bottom of the screen:
#1 Suspect, and I thought,
Maybe I'll buy a baby,

the kind from an orphanage
UNICEF tells me exists elsewhere,
where I'll send a monthly check
in exchange for a pencil-printed letter
on embellished stationary
and a water-stained photo
of a six-year-old standing on a dirt mound
with stringy hair, a round middle,
and a toothless smile.
Maybe I'll find my baby
when they post a picture of it on TV
like the man in the Tigers cap.

There's a sea of dads 100 feet, a strip search,
and a pat down away. When the officer summoned me
to check in and called me *Sugar*, I did not wince.
I couldn't be angry.
That's my name, isn't it?

MEMOIR

I check my pockets

for errant quarters or ChapStick tubes

as I approach the subway turnstile

I tie back my hair

ready my driver's license

before remembering I am not going to prison

today, today I can carry anything

ABANDONED AMBIGUITY STUDY

We visited Manzanar on our way to Death Valley, laughed at our hair frizzing in the humid heat, asked my cousin's husband if his parents ever talked about their time here. *They didn't talk much about anything.* He jogged ahead to catch his youngest from the sidewalk curb.

Before kids, he'd taught history, but he never learned Japanese. His parents couldn't teach what they'd been taught not to speak.

When I teach APA style to students fresh out of prison, I admit, *This grammar reflects White Supremacy, as scholars forge the rules, developed in the racist lineage of Western academia, by which we are expected to write and speak.* I advise, *Don't let them find more reason to discount you. Before you get creative, you must prove you can pick up what we teach.*

At fifteen, I went to Costa Rica to help a village's infrastructure "catch up to the times." Wells and walls and such. The villagers whispered amongst themselves as they watched us stir concrete and husband dirt plots over many days what they'd have done in hours. *Our history spans decades!* the organization had listed. *We serve communities historically underserved around the world!* Each morning, the choppy, hour-long crawl up the mountain from our resort to the village, singing along to Tracy Chapman through strained van speakers: *Don't you know, talkin' bout a revolution…*

As ever, headlines like *Families Split at Southern Border* plaster the collective mind, teaching people like me what my family has always warned could become of us again. The rules keep changing: who to catch and send away, or keep, or kill.

Of course I've been scared. Of course I've caught a student's eye and thought, *I would not want to be alone with you.* Some history's irrelevant and some is not. I too have abided a close friend's pleading, *Don't you ever tell*, upon disclosing something unforgiveable.

In broken grade-school Spanish I'd flirted with the Costa Rican teens, fellow volunteers with colones in our pockets, walking cool up to the bodega for paletas de hielo in vibrant pinks and greens.

At the Manzanar museum, a woman gave a talk on her time as a kid in the camp. *Don't you understand? Us kids, we had fun. All our friends were there.*

I can't say I've not done unforgiveable things myself.

UPON BEING TOLD I'M UNTRUSTWORTHY
with a line from "Catalogue of Grief" by Aria Aber

How can a Jew write a book about prison
— Without mentioning Palestine —

I who cannot read from right to left
I don't know where I come from

How America's "Indian" Reservations
— Inspired Hitler's Auschwitz —

Or Abu Ghraib and those soldiers, barely twenty
Thumbs raised in the air, smiles wide

As if they'd just won a game of beer pong
— Had they been in college instead —

— The conclusive flower-growing-through-cement —
— Concrete wall —

— Barbed wire fence —
— Trite unless — no —

— Until —
— It is yours —

A baby's cry the same

The world over—I

*A baby cries
for her father, who,
holding her, soothes,*
I'm already here.

I'm already here.

ARS POETICA
after Hermes, tr. from Arabic by Maged Zaher

I want a poetry
that reassembles the body

that is

investigates love
how it is not enough

that is

what prison taught me
teaches me

that is

I want to not be lonely

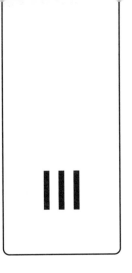

count the nights you lay awake waiting
count the nights you lay awake wondering
count the ways you rewrote the ending

—C.D. WRIGHT

REVISION

There were days I saw myself a peach and told him so, wrote
ripeness so thick I'd have to close my notebook
and walk, hours, sublimating, hours or else not

sublimate and write him, right after, of flesh, its impossible
later summer ready, my late summer indulgence. Now I think *idle*
not *excess*, not *endless, fervent, urgent*, not *I will die*

of infinite want which drives the infinite want which I thought then,
those days curled in my bed meditating on the miles
between his and mine, meaningless in light

of the prison's absoluteness, independent
from any physical traveling towards.
That summer I meant *I need* and said *everything*

and thought *if only* and *then* and *then* and *then.*
I knew better than to imagine an arrival
but imagined an arrival, knowing an after

must follow but the after became an unliving thing
those days when ready was an end, no risk of loss,
no rot. Ready meant the end of want, I thought.

I sent a letter thinking he could feel my tremble in the letter,
that unliving thing made living with enough desire.
All that my heart longs for,

fulfill, sang Sappho, desire's servant
or, sometimes, chef, if you believe that longing can be fed,
wrested by the object of its reaching only when the object reached.

If you believe that longing can be fed, wrested
by the object of its reaching if only reached, you are like me,
how I was, then, when I thought abandoning the reach

meant longing won, a hunger so complete and permanent
and empty in the shape of him. How cute
to think the yearning due to that, a man so fully locked away

the poems—so ripe—could almost write themselves.
When it ended, it didn't end, the letters stopped
but not the longing which, I'm learning, in the months

and years now gone, is a most natural occurrence.
Almost capitalist if it weren't so full of feeling: believing
that a thing once gained will heal what is innate. Insatiable,

the peach wanting water and sun, and falling
if not plucked in time. The branch will bear again,
probably. The remnants of the fruit dissolve, no

fruit-shaped hole left in the soil. The me that holds
the him-shaped hole I picture deep inside my body
is just me holding my body. The want just human.

Kneeling.

NOTES

11 ||| UNIDENTIFIED MATERIAL RESIDUE is repurposed from the Michigan Department of Corrections (MDOC) Correctional Facilities Administration *Family Information Packet*. The last line is after Zora Neale Hurston.

12 ||| "A name is just a room you can't get out of" is after Joshua Jennifer Espinoza.

24 ||| "Buying a Vending Card Before the Visit" refers to the MDOC prohibition of bringing cash or coins into the visiting room. Due to this rule, visitors must buy a special debit-like card from a machine in the waiting room to use in the visiting room if they wish to purchase food or beverages from the vending machines when visiting their prisoner.

35 ||| "The body and its bony cage of law" is from "An Explanation of America" by Robert Pinsky, from the book of the same title.

45 ||| This palindromic form is inspired by "Myth" by Natasha Trethewey.

47 ||| "FREELAND: An Erasure" is an erasure of letters written to the author by friend and incarcerated writer Justin Rovillos Monson between 2014 and 2017.

67 ||| The image of a "tightrope to the moon" is after the painting *Elephant on a Tightrope* by Free Ray Gray, on display at the *2016 Annual Exhibition of Michigan Prisoner Art*.

This image can be found at the following URL:
https://dcc.carceralstateproject.lsa.umich.edu/s/pcapartdatabase/item/34027

66 ||| The concept for this poem was inspired by Claudia Rankine.

69 ||| "In Which the Prisoner Paints Himself as Rembrandt" describes the painting "Dear Anonymous" by the incarcerated artist Montney, sold to the author at the *2014 Annual Exhibition of Michigan Prisoner Art*.

This image can be found at the following URL:
https://dcc.carceralstateproject.lsa.umich.edu/s/pcapartdatabase/item/25138

82 ||| The author thanks Leila Chatti, whose prompts during a summer workshop catalyzed this poem.

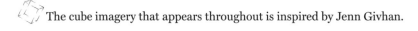 The cube imagery that appears throughout is inspired by Jenn Givhan.

ACKNOWLEDGEMENTS

Thank you, deeply, to the publications in which the following poems (some in earlier versions) appeared:

128 Lit — "Ars Poetica"
Epiphany Literary Magazine — "The Commune in Santa Cruz"
Fence — "Phone Call with the Now Formerly Beloved, November 2016"
Honey Literary — "Inheritance" and "CORRECTIONS"
The Journal — "Autobiography"
jubilat — "At the group home where I work"
The Margins — "Security"
Only Poems — "[The prison photographer makes his rounds,];" "ode to phone sex;" and "Self on Psych Hold Imagines Future Self After Psych Hold"
Pleiades Magazine — "Upon Being Told I'm Untrustworthy"
Poetry Magazine — "FREELAND: An Erasure"
Pigeon Pages — "Visiting Standards" and "Ontology of My Assumed Immunity"
Radar Poetry — "In the Waiting Room (flashback)"
Saranac Review — "[I only ever see him in a jumpsuit]"
Split This Rock (Poem of the Week) — "Bone Tumor"
Tupelo Quarterly — "Grand Unified Theory of Mass Incarceration, or, How to Leave;" "Phenomenology;" "[(What were you thinking]" and "[A number is just a name.]"
West Branch — "Repression" and "To Be"

"[My friend Will is trying to get better at writing.]" was included in Poet Tree Town, an Ann Arbor Poetry Month project in which poems were posted publicly in multiple locations throughout Ann Arbor, MI.

ACKNOWLEDGEMENTS, TOO

"... nobody, / But nobody / Can make it out here alone."
—Maya Angelou

Thank you to my earliest writing teachers: my parents, who gave me journals to scribble in at three; my sister, always the writer in the family; and Eileen Bigham, who shepherded my first stories into the world.

Thank you, Carey Salerno, Alyssa Neptune, Emily Marquis, Genevieve Hartman, Lacey Dunham, Trevor Ketner, and everyone at Alice James Books for providing such a dreamy debut author experience.

Thank you Ayla Zuraw-Friedland and the Frances Goldin Literary Agency, whose belief in my work made this book right here possible.

Thank you, Justin, without whom this book wouldn't, couldn't exist.

Thank you to my colleagues, peers, fellow writers from NYU (an incomplete list): Diannely Antigua, Dominique Béchard, Chase Berggrun, Matthew Brailas, Izzi Conner, Sean DesVignes, b ferguson, Ethan Fortuna, Sophia Holtz, John Liles, Yuxi Lin, Kyle Carrero Lopez, Wally Ludel, Nadra Mabrouk, Momina Mela, Henry Mills, Vanessa Moody, Madeleine Mori, Ryan Ouimet, Catherine Pikula, Mal Profeta, Karisma Price, Jess Rizkallah, Marney Rathbun, Sahar Romani, T.J. Smith, J.J. Starr, Eleanor Wright, Crystal Valentine, Phil West, and Alexandra Zukerman. Special thanks to Aria Aber, Rachel Mannheimer, and Maggie Millner, who comprised the most intimidating and inspiring thesis cohort the universe could conjure.

Thank you to my writing friends & colleagues I know from beyond the ivory tower: Ashna Ali, Sarah Ghazal Ali, Tamar Ashdot, Elly Belle, Rosebud Ben-Oni, Jiordan Castle, Dorothy Chan, Phil Christman, Jesse Rice-Evans, Andrew Felsher, Shelby Handler, Shelli Hoppe, Karan Kapoor, You Li, Robert Wood Lynn, Mordecai Martin, Shannan Mann, Caits Meissner, Rita Mookerjee, Nila Narain, Isaac Pickell, Share Roman, Dan Schapiro, Gabi Shiner, H.R. Webster, Monica Wendel, and Katie Zeitz.

Thank you to my writing teachers and supporters, those I personally know: Catherine Barnett, Leila Chatti, Angel Dominguez, Jenn Givhan, Kimiko Hahn, Ed Hirsch, Major Jackson, Ken Mikolowski, Sharon Olds, Meghan O'Rourke, Maggie Queeney, Anastasia Reneé, Martha Silano, Jeanine Walker, David Wagoner, Rebecca Wolff, Shelley Wong; and those I have yet, or never had a chance, to meet, but whose works and legacies inspire me deeply: Elizabeth Bishop, CAConrad, Frantz Fanon, Michel Foucault, bell hooks, Marie Howe, Edmond Jabès, A. Van Jordan, Etheridge Knight, Shane McCrae, Toni Morrison, Claudia Rankine, Srikanth Reddy, Muriel Rukeyser, Solmaz Sharif, Layli Long Soldier, Judith Tannenbaum, C.D. Wright, Maged Zaher... And, thanks to Nana Kwame Adjei-Brenyah, whom I have not yet met but who lovingly reminds us literary competition is unnecessary when we are all working and writing for liberation.

Special thanks to Anne Carson, Bob Curry, Geoffrey Nutter, and Matt Rohrer for your astounding generosity and support during and after my time at NYU.

Thank you to friends, colleagues, and inspirations on the front lines of abolition work: Michelle Alexander, Hala Alyan, Angela Davis, Brittany Hailer, C. Davida Ingram, Spoon Jackson, Fady Joudah, Victoria Law, Ashley Lucas, Heather Martin, E. Ethelbert Miller, Robbie Moore, Nikkita Oliver, Molly Pearl, Kathy Robinson, Amani Sawari, Bennett Stein, Rafaela Varela, Marshall Thomas, Heather Ann Thompson and Rachael Zafer.

Thank you to my friends and inspirations who showed me I could be an artist: Caitlin Brzezinski, Will Chang, Alice Gosti, Ryan Law, Darrell Jones, Dr. Nancy Ambrose King, Lylli Meredith, Mark Murray, Michaela Ravasio, Christina Robson, Nola Sporn Smith, and Erin Wiley.

Thank you to my friends and colleagues at *Commonplace*: Lola Anaya, Christine

Larusso, and, of course, Rachel Zucker. You've welcomed me into a poetry world filled with energy, awe, and chutzpah—a winning combination.

Thank you to my oldest, dearest friends, who care not if I ever write again (this is a relief, not a condemnation): Carolyn Blessing, Renee Gross, Shang Kong, Jenna Spinei, and Katie Wahl.

Thank you, Andrew, for supporting, encouraging, asking, loving, supporting, supporting, and supporting again.

Thank you, and infinite love, to all those in carceral institutions, and to your friends, family, and loved ones, for all you do to support your people.

And thank you, dear reader, for trusting me with language and your time.

A free reader's guide, with questions for reflection
and further inquiry, is available at the following link:
alicejamesbooks.org/freeland-readers-guide.

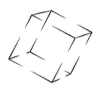

RECENT TITLES FROM ALICE JAMES BOOKS

Mothersalt, Mia Ayumi Malhotra
When the Horses, Mary Helen Callier
Cold Thief Place, Esther Lin
If Nothing, Matthew Nienow
Zombie Vomit Mad Libs, Duy Đoàn
The Holy & Broken Bliss, Alicia Ostriker
Wish Ave, Alessandra Lynch
Autobiomythography of, Ayokunle Falomo
Old Stranger: Poems, Joan Larkin
I Don't Want To Be Understood, Joshua Jennifer Espinoza
Canandaigua, Donald Revell
In the Days That Followed, Kevin Goodan
Light Me Down: The New & Collected Poems of Jean Valentine, Jean Valentine
Song of My Softening, Omotara James
Theophanies, Sarah Ghazal Ali
Orders of Service, Willie Lee Kinard III
The Dead Peasant's Handbook, Brian Turner
The Goodbye World Poem, Brian Turner
The Wild Delight of Wild Things, Brian Turner
I Am the Most Dangerous Thing, Candace Williams
Burning Like Her Own Planet, Vandana Khanna
Standing in the Forest of Being Alive, Katie Farris
Feast, Ina Cariño
Decade of the Brain: Poems, Janine Joseph
American Treasure, Jill McDonough
We Borrowed Gentleness, J. Estanislao Lopez
Brother Sleep, Aldo Amparán
Sugar Work, Katie Marya
Museum of Objects Burned by the Souls in Purgatory, Jeffrey Thomson
Constellation Route, Matthew Olzmann
How to Not Be Afraid of Everything, Jane Wong
Brocken Spectre, Jacques J. Rancourt
No Ruined Stone, Shara McCallum
The Vault, Andrés Cerpa
White Campion, Donald Revell

Alice James Books is committed to publishing books that matter. The press was founded in 1973 in Boston, Massachusetts to give women access to publishing. As a cooperative, authors performed the day-to-day undertakings of the press. The press continues to expand and grow from its formative roots, guided by its founding values of access, excellence, inclusivity, and collaboration in publishing. Its mission is to publish books that matter and preserve a place of belonging for poets who inspire us. AJB seeks to broaden our collective interpretation of what constitutes the American poetic voice and is dedicated to helping its artists achieve purposeful engagement with broad audiences and communities nationwide. The press was named for Alice James, sister to William and Henry, whose extraordinary gift for writing went unrecognized during her lifetime.

Designed by Tiani Kennedy

Printed by Versa Press